GUGLIELMO
MARCONI

Richard Tames

Franklin Watts
London • New York • Sydney • Toronto

Contents

The Dreamer	4
Electromagnetic Waves	6
The Experimenter	7
The Inventor	9
A Royal Encounter	12
Across the Atlantic	13
The Businessman	16
The *Titanic*	19
The Soldier and Diplomat	20
Elettra	24
The Statesman	26
Find Out More ...	30
Glossary	31
Index	32

© 1990 Franklin Watts

First published in Great Britain
in 1990 by
Franklin Watts
96 Leonard Street
London EC2

First published in the USA by
Franklin Watts Inc.
387 Park Avenue South
New York
N.Y. 10016

First published in Australia by
Franklin Watts
14 Mars Road
Lane Cove
NSW 2066

UK ISBN: 0 7496 0128 0

Phototypeset by: JB Type, Hove, East Sussex
Printed in: Belgium
Series Editor: Hazel Poole
Editor: Dee Turner
Designed by: Nick Cannan

A CIP catalogue record for this book is available from
the British Library.

The Dreamer

Guglielmo Marconi became famous throughout the world as the inventor of **radio** communication and an important public figure, but little in his childhood suggested that he would make much of himself. Born in 1874, he was the son of a wealthy Italian father and a strong-willed Irish mother. His father thought Guglielmo was often a bit of a nuisance, but his mother saw him as an amusing companion to be indulged and shown off. When he was just three years old, she took him on a three-year visit to England, where his elder brother was at school. Guglielmo spent two years at a private school in Bedford. When he finally started school in Italy he spoke Italian hesitantly and with a foreign accent. His life there was a misery, as he was insulted by his teachers and teased by his classmates. The only good things to come out of this time were a life-long friend — Luigi Solari — and learning to sail a boat and play the piano, both of which Guglielmo Marconi did very well.

Although he was not very good at school subjects, he had a lively and inventive mind. He was always amusing himself by making things out of any odd bits and pieces he found lying about the Villa Grifone, his father's country estate near Bologna. Once, he converted his English cousin Daisy's sewing-machine into a **spit** for roasting meat. Another time he rigged up an arrangement of wires and a battery to make an electric bell. But when he failed to qualify for entry to the Italian Naval Academy, his father was furious, and thought he should be devoting himself to serious study.

In 1887, when he was thirteen, Guglielmo entered the Leghorn Technical Institute. There he at once began to take a passionate interest in physics and chemistry. His mother paid for private lessons from a Professor Rosa, who introduced

Guglielmo (left) **with his Irish mother, Annie (née Jameson) and his elder brother, Alfonso.**

him to the mysteries of electricity. Yet, some years later, he failed the entrance examination to Bologna University. Once more his influential mother stepped in and got permission from Professor Righi, one of Italy's leading scientists, for her son to use Bologna University laboratory facilities and to read books from the university library.

Another important influence was a retired **telegraph** operator whom he met by chance in Leghorn. The old man was nearly blind, so

By the time he was in his twenties, Marconi was already recognized as the world's leading expert on radio.

Marconi used to read aloud to him. In return, the old man taught him **Morse code**. Although he could not even suspect it, Marconi was gaining the practical skills and the theoretical knowledge that would one day enable him to take a fundamental step forward in the area that had become his obsession — electricity.

Electromagnetic Waves

In 1864, a young Scottish scientist, James Clerk-Maxwell (1831–79), suggested that there were such things as electromagnetic waves. You could not hear or see them, but they were, he suggested, like sound waves and had a measurable **frequency** and length. They were different from sound, however, in that they travelled at the speed of light and could pass through gases, liquids, solids and even a vacuum, where no air existed.

The existence of these waves was not proved until 1887, when the German scientist, Heinrich Hertz (1857–94) showed that the theory was correct. Hertz built a transmitter made of a coil of wire connected to an electricity supply of high voltage, and two metal bars facing each other. When he pressed the key to turn on the high voltage, a crackling spark of electricity jumped across the gap between the bars. When he put a similar spark-gap apparatus some metres away to act as a receiver, a tiny spark jumped across the spark-gap of the receiver. This showed that electromagnetic waves from the transmitter had been radiated to the receiver.

It was this work that inspired Marconi to carry on an investigation into electromagnetic waves — which became known as Hertzian waves.

Hertz (left) **was a pupil of Hermann von Helmholtz, whose electrical experiments inspired Bell to invent the telephone. Maxwell** (right) **published his first scientific paper at 14 and also produced one of the world's first colour photographs.**

The Experimenter

In 1894, twenty-year-old Marconi was on holiday in the Alps when he read about the death of the German scientist, Heinrich Hertz. He also read about the work Hertz had done on the mysterious electromagnetic waves. Almost at once Marconi decided to try to use these waves as a way of sending messages through the air — a kind of telegraph, but one that did not involve wires. It would be **"wireless"** telegraphy, or radio as we would now call it. He later remembered:

"The idea obsessed me more and more in those mountains … I worked it out in imagination. I did not attempt any experiments until we returned to the Villa Grifone in the autumn, but then two large rooms at the top of the house were set aside for me by my mother. And there I began experiments in earnest."

Professor Righi, not surprisingly, told him his chances of success were slim. Righi had worked for many years trying hard to understand electromagnetic waves. If Italy's leading expert had failed, how could a young man who couldn't even get into university succeed? But Marconi was determined.

He began by repeating Hertz's experiments. However, unlike Righi and other experimenters, Marconi was not interested in abstract science. He wanted to use Hertzian waves to send messages. He did not even know that Oliver Lodge had already done this in England. But Lodge, having shown that it was possible to send messages over distances of some metres, lost all interest in the matter. Marconi's main effort really began where Lodge left off — trying to increase the distance over which messages could be sent.

Marconi's efforts were greatly helped by a major improvement in the design of the receiver. The small spark-gap of Hertz's original receiver had been replaced by a much more sensitive detector called a Branly **coherer**, a glass tube

Sir Oliver Lodge (1851–1940) turned from radio to psychic research.

containing iron filings and with an electrical contact at each end. When the receiving coil, connected to the coherer, picked up electromagnetic radiation, the filings stuck together (cohered). This reduced the electrical resistance between the two contacts. Because the coherer was connected to a battery, the fall in resistance caused a surge in current which could be used to sound a buzzer or make a Morse code machine print a mark. In other words, the tiny amount of electromagnetic energy picked up by the receiver was not itself needed to create any signal. Instead it was used to stimulate a much more powerful electrical source, which in turn created the signal.

By the end of 1894, Marconi was able to demonstrate to his mother that he could press a key at one end of the attic and sound a buzzer 9 m (30 ft) away, without any wires connecting the two. By the summer of the following year he was patiently improving his apparatus to enable it to send signals much further. By trial and error he greatly improved the coherer, altering its shape and adjusting the mixture of iron filings. By chance, moving the different parts of a modified receiver

about, he discovered the principle of the **aerial** and the **earth**, and was suddenly able to send much more powerful signals for distances of over a kilometre. Marconi recognized at once the practical importance of this accidental breakthrough.

He had got as far as he could on his own, and he knew it. He needed better equipment, technical assistance, and money to develop his amusing toy into a practical technology. Marconi's father, who was now taking his son very seriously, approached influential local friends, who in turn approached the Italian government's postal ministry. The ministry was not interested. Marconi's mother approached influential friends in England. England *was* interested. In February 1896, Annie and Guglielmo arrived in London.

Marconi, shortly after his arrival in England.

The Inventor

Marconi's expedition to Britain began unhappily when customs officers damaged his apparatus in the course of "examining" it. They did not know what it was and were unable to make much sense of his answers when he told them. Marconi gave no public demonstration of his apparatus in London until he had filed a provisional **patent** to prevent anyone from stealing his ideas. So it was not until July that Marconi, having privately demonstrated his invention to William Preece, the Chief Engineer of the Post Office, was invited to show it off to an invited audience of engineers and government officials on the roof of the General Post Office building in London.

Using a Morse printer, Marconi successfully sent messages to a receiving point, manned by Preece's staff, on the roof of another Post Office building. The distance was less than 1.6 km (1 mile) but there were several tall buildings blocking the view between the two points. The audience was suitably impressed. At the end of the demonstration Preece turned to Marconi and said "Young man, you have done something truly exceptional. I congratulate you on it."

Preece then arranged for a bigger demonstration to be held on Salisbury Plain, a flat, open area in Wiltshire that was often used by the army for manoeuvres. The demonstration took place on 2 September in the presence of representatives of the War Office and the Admiralty, as well as more Post Office engineers. Afterwards it was officially reported that:

" ... the general results of the experiments conclusively show that the whole system is well worthy of further consideration and trial."

In December 1896, Preece and Marconi together presented a lecture-demonstration for the benefit of the Press and the general public. Preece stood on the platform of the hall, pressing a transmitting key in a black box, while Marconi walked around the hall with a receiver, also inside a black box. As Preece signalled, a bell inside Marconi's box rang. The onlookers

Post Office engineers with Marconi apparatus, Bristol Channel, England, 1897.

An elegantly-dressed Marconi shows his radio to Italian naval officers.

were stunned by this modest theatrical trick.

In March 1897, further trials on Salisbury Plain saw Marconi transmit signals over distances of 7 km (4.3 miles), using kites and balloons to lift aerials into the air. In May he achieved another "first", transmitting over water — 14 km (8.7 miles) across the Bristol Channel.

Marconi's success did not go unnoticed in Italy, and the Italian Navy soon saw how useful a wireless system would be for ship-to-shore communication. After all, ships could not trail telegraph wires behind them!

Both the Italian authorities and Marconi himself knew that, as an Italian citizen, he was liable for military service. But Marconi wanted to stay in England to continue his experiments with Post Office support and to raise money to establish a company to develop his invention. Marconi's British relatives suggested he should become a British citizen. His mother, after all, was British already and he spoke the language fluently. He would then have no obligations to the Italian military authorities.

Marconi, however, was a strong supporter of his native country and would only consider renouncing his Italian citizenship as a very last

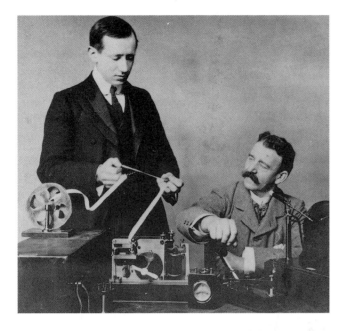

Marconi with Kemp, a loyal, lifelong assistant.

resort. In his dilemma he contacted the Italian Ambassador in London. The diplomat came up with an ingenious solution which benefited everyone. Marconi was enrolled in the Italian Navy and posted immediately as an assistant naval **attaché** to the London Embassy. All he had to do was continue with his scientific work. Marconi showed his appreciation of this kindness by donating his naval pay to the funds of the Italian Hospital in London.

As a member of the Italian Navy, however, Marconi could not refuse an invitation to return to Italy to demonstrate his new invention. So, in July 1897, he visited his homeland and sent a message from one floor of the Ministry of Marine to the next; tactfully he made it "Viva l'Italia" (Long Live Italy). The following day he was presented to the King and Queen of Italy, who congratulated him on his invention. For weeks he carried out experiments at the dockyard at Spezia, sending messages between ships and the shore. Here he discovered something very important: wireless messages could be sent even when a ship was below the horizon and out of sight of land.

By the time Marconi arrived back in London, his English backers had set up "The Wireless Telegraph and Signal Company Limited". In return for granting the company the rights to all his patents, Marconi was made a director and given 60 per cent of the shares, plus almost £15,000 in cash. It was just three years since he had begun his experiments in the attic. They had made him famous. Now they had made him rich as well. And he was still only 23 years old.

The balanced crystal receiver. Note the company name and patent numbers.

A Royal Encounter

Queen Victoria herself was impressed with Marconi's success. If Marconi could transmit from ship to shore, he could also transmit from shore to ship. The shore in this case was Osborne House, the Queen's holiday home on the Isle of Wight, and the ship was a yacht, moored off the island, where her middle-aged son, the Prince of Wales, was recovering from a knee injury. Although he was 57 years old, the Queen still treated him like a naughty boy. She saw Signor Marconi's apparatus as the way to receive daily news on the progress of the royal knee. Would Signor Marconi set up a wireless apparatus for the Queen? Signor Marconi, knowing the value of royal support, most certainly would. He did so, and over the course of the summer, 160 messages were passed between the Queen and her son.

One day, Marconi was in the grounds of Osborne House, inspecting the aerial that he had erected there. A gardener told him not to go through a certain area in case he disturbed the Queen, but Marconi ignored him. When the incident was reported to Queen Victoria she exclaimed dismissively "Get another electrician." "Alas, your Majesty," came the reply, "England has no Marconi." Intrigued, the Queen asked to meet the young genius and congratulated him on the success of the link with her son's yacht.

Queen Victoria using more traditional communications at Osborne House, her favourite residence. Her son made it a naval academy when he became King.

Marconi's company began to set up wireless stations in Britain to conduct further trials. The first were built on the Isle of Wight and, nearby on the south coast, at Poole in Dorset. Marconi himself conducted endless tests at sea to improve transmissions between ship and shore. It was exhausting work and in storms it was dangerous as well as very wet. But it proved that wireless telegraphy could be made to work in all weathers.

During 1898 and 1899, wireless began to prove its practical value in a variety of ways. It was used to summon a lifeboat to two shipping accidents, and it supplied a reporting service on the movement of ships for the insurers at Lloyd's of London. But the general public was far more impressed by Marconi's ability to supply minute-by-minute reports of the Kingstown yacht races for the Dublin *Daily Express*, broadcasting them from a sea-drenched tug-boat trailing behind the race. Marconi was so pleased with the newspaper coverage that he even had an Italian version of it published in his home town of Bologna.

In the spring of 1899, Marconi arranged the world's first international radio transmission, between the southern coast of England and the northern coast of France, a distance of about 50 km (31 miles). In July of the same year, three British warships were equipped with Marconi wireless apparatus for the summer manoeuvres and regularly communicated with one another over distances of nearly 100 km (62 miles).

The Marconi Company was soon offering commercial users a wireless system that worked. A factory was set up to make wireless apparatus, but it received virtually no orders and needed money for further

The aerial system at Poldhu, Cornwall 1901 — before the storm (left) **and after** (right).

investment. Undeterred, Marconi and his partners set up a separate "Marconi International Marine Communication Company Limited" to provide a service to merchant shipping. But first it needed a chain of shore stations to send and receive messages, and that meant more expense. At this moment, when everything seemed strained to breaking-point, Marconi astounded his fellow directors by announcing that he intended to build two new stations, more powerful than any previously constructed, to send messages all the way across the Atlantic Ocean.

This seemed like sheer madness. The distance was over twenty times greater than anything previously attempted, and the curvature of the earth meant that, in effect, there would be a mountain of water 320 km (200 miles) high between the transmitter and receiver. But Marconi insisted that it could and should be done. His fellow directors agreed to build the necessary sites at Poldhu in Cornwall (England) and Cape Cod in Massachusetts (United States).

A ring of aerial masts, 61 m (200 ft) high, was erected at Poldhu, only to be wrecked by a gale on 17 September, 1901. A stronger structure was built in its place within a week. Then the Cape Cod station suffered a similar disaster. Marconi bowed to fate, altered his plans and decided instead to send one-way communication between Poldhu and St. John's, Newfoundland, the nearest point to

Marconi (left) **supervises the raising of a kite aerial at Newfoundland, 1901.**

About to prove the impossible —
Marconi with transatlantic test
equipment, 1901.

Britain in North America. He decided to use kites and balloons to raise the receiving aerial.

Bad weather led to the complete loss of a balloon when Marconi and his team first tried raising an aerial on 11 December. The next day a kite was lost. A second attempt was more successful, though the aerial bucked and reared in the strong wind. Marconi swore that he heard faint "dot-dot-dot" signals, the pre-arranged Morse "S", on three separate occasions in the course of two hours. Before he could improve on this effort, worse weather closed in and brought the tests to an end.

Marconi claimed success for his transatlantic transmission, despite the lack of any witness to confirm his achievement. The public was enthusiastic about the news, but some scientists were sceptical. Nobody doubted Marconi's honesty, but perhaps he heard only what he desperately wanted to hear? Perhaps he heard random noises made by crackling atmospheric **static**, not deliberate signals?

Two months later, however, Marconi finally silenced the doubters by rigging up an outsize aerial on a westbound liner which enabled it to receive messages from Poldhu at a range of nearly 2,500 km (1,550 miles).

The Businessman

It seemed at first that radio's most promising business use lay in helping ships at sea keep in touch with the shore. In 1900, the first merchant ship was fitted with Marconi equipment — the German liner *Kaiser Wilhelm der Grosse*. By 1902 there were 70 ships with wireless equipment, and 25 land stations with which they could communicate about weather conditions, shipping movements and emergencies.

In 1905, Marconi, who was now 31, married nineteen-year-old Beatrice (Bea) O'Brien. Like his mother, she was a member of the Irish Protestant upper-classes. She may well have felt deceived by her new husband's charm when she found herself living in a small wooden house in the wilds of Nova Scotia, Canada, while he struggled all day and half the night with the technical problems of re-equipping a wireless station with a new aerial. He then went off to Clifden in a remote part of western Ireland to supervise the construction of the most powerful wireless station yet built.

By 1907, six years after his first experimental transmission, Marconi was at last able to offer a commercial transatlantic message service in competition with the telegraph. The Marconi Company's finances were in a rocky state. Some managers were having to work unpaid and many workers had to be dismissed. Only

Beatrice O'Brien — an Irish aristocrat, like Marconi's mother.

Marconi's own money kept the company afloat, and then, when the managing director resigned, Marconi himself took his place. Fortunately, the appointment of the very able Godfrey Isaacs to that position in 1910 brought efficiency to the company, and allowed Marconi to get back to his researches.

If business life was stressful for

Marconi (third from left) **with staff of Glace Bay station, Canada, 1908 and dwarfed by the Clifden capacitor** (right).

Marconi, there were compensations. In 1908, Bea presented him with a baby daughter, Degna. One day she would grow up to write his biography, called *My Father, Marconi*. In 1909, science honoured him with the award of the Nobel Prize for Physics. Ironically, he shared it with the German Professor K. F. Braun, one of the founders of Telefunken, the Marconi Company's main European rival.

Marconi looked now for fresh fields to conquer, so he proposed an ambitious Imperial Wireless Scheme to link the various countries of the British Empire with a network of radio stations. Marconi promised to send messages at half the price charged by telegraph companies — an immense benefit for businesses. But the government saw that wireless would give the Navy a **strategic** advantage. Telegraph cables, whether on land or under the sea, could be cut in time of war. Radio waves could not. And a global communications network centred on London would enable the Admiralty to co-ordinate the movements of the entire Royal Navy worldwide. It was a tempting vision. The British Government was uneasy about placing so much power in the hands of a privately owned company, but British defence experts wanted to have radio, and only the Marconi Company was capable of building the wireless stations. So, in 1912, a contract was negotiated for the first six. The Company would be paid for building them and receive a royalty on the traffic they carried, but the stations themselves would be State-owned.

Souvenirs (above) **of 1909 Nobel Prize winners shows medal.**
(Below) **Marconi with Kemp and Page.**

The *Titanic*

The *Titanic*, the world's greatest ocean liner, was said to be unsinkable. However, on her maiden voyage across the Atlantic, she struck an iceberg at 11.40 pm on Sunday, 14 April, 1912, and sank within three hours. Her radio operator's calls for help were heard by the liner *Carpathia* some 96 km (60 miles) away, and so about 700 passengers were rescued. But many of the 1500 who died might have been saved if the ship nearest the stricken liner, the *California*, had also picked up her distress calls. But the *California* had only one radio operator, who had just gone off duty. Another complication was that the *Titanic*'s distress calls led to a sort of traffic jam of radio messages between other shipping, picking up the news, querying it, confirming it and offering to help. Not until 24 hours after the event was it known ashore that she had definitely sunk.

The British government held an enquiry into the disaster. In giving expert evidence, Marconi suggested there should be an "auto-alarm" that would ring a bell in response to distress signals, even if the radio was not manned at the time. In 1920, the Marconi Company demonstrated such a device, which later became compulsory for certain types of ship.

Strangely, both Marconi and his wife had been invited as guests on the *Titanic*'s tragic voyage. An important business appointment in the United States made Marconi change his booking to another ship, but Beatrice changed her mind only at the last minute when their two-year-old son was taken ill.

Radio cabin (above) **of** *SS Lusitania* **(1907). The** *Titanic*'s **similar equipment helped to save at least some of her passengers.**

The Soldier and Diplomat

The contract for an Imperial Wireless Scheme put Marconi's name in the history books in a way he could never have foreseen, and most certainly never deserved. While the contract was waiting to be confirmed by the House of Commons, gossip in financial circles of the City of London was picked up by the newspapers. It was alleged that the contract had been awarded as a result of bribery and that certain government ministers had used their confidential knowledge of the negotiations to buy and sell shares in the Marconi Company to make money for themselves. A Select Committee was appointed to investigate what immediately became known as "the Marconi Scandal". The Committee found that there was no evidence whatever of bribery, and that although certain ministers had acted unwisely and perhaps dishonourably, they had done nothing criminal. Marconi himself was never at any point accused of wrongdoing, but he was extremely bitter that his name should have been involved in the whole wretched business. Eventually a new contract was signed in July 1913, but none of the projected six stations was ready when World War I broke out in August 1914, so the whole scheme was abandoned.

1912 was remarkable for two other events touching Marconi, apart from the *Titanic* disaster. One was a triumph, the other a tragedy. The first was the construction of an entirely new factory at Chelmsford, Essex, in less than six months. The second was a motor accident while he and his wife were on a working holiday in Italy. A head-on smash with another car so severely damaged Marconi's right eye that it had to be completely removed. After a frightening period of total blindness, he regained the sight of his left eye.

Proud father — Marconi with infant daughter Degna. (Right) **On active service in the Great War — Marconi** (centre) **in uniform.**

In July 1914, Marconi was honoured by Britain when King George V made him a Knight Grand Cross of the Royal Victorian Order, an honour that can only be given by the sovereign. A month later, Britain was at war. Marconi, as a foreigner, found he was not able to travel freely in the country that he had come to regard as his home. Italy was, however, a **neutral** state when the conflict broke out and so Marconi was allowed to return to Rome to live.

When Italy entered the war on the Allied side in 1915, Marconi at once joined the forces as an expert adviser on radio. Unsure of where or how best to use him, the authorities at first made him a lieutenant in the Army and then a lieutenant-commander in the Navy. His chief technical contribution during the war was to work out a system of ultra-short-wave communication which could be used by warships directly in line of sight of one another. This relieved the overcrowding of traffic on "normal" wavebands, which was confusing communications in the restricted Mediterranean area.

Later in the war, Marconi's international fame led him to undertake various public relations tasks on behalf of the Italian government. In 1917, when the United States entered the war, he was sent to America as a member of a "good-will mission". He knew the country well from business trips and had had personal contact with many of its most influential leaders. He was also extremely popular among the large Italian immigrant community. He made two official visits to London in 1918. These activities had little to do with wireless but they were certainly about communications. Marconi radiated charm and confidence on behalf of his country. You might say he was one of the best ambassadors Italy never had.

Marconi, the diplomat (below) **kept a copy of the famous 1905 "Spy" cartoon** (right) **framed on his mantlepiece.**

Elettra

Marconi had never lost his boyhood love of sailing, and his own use of wireless to report on ocean racing fuelled his ambition to possess a yacht of his own. He enjoyed the high life, and an ocean-going cruiser would enable him to entertain in style. At the same time it could have a serious scientific purpose. Fitted with a laboratory, it could easily serve as a mobile base, going wherever an experiment needed to be done. It would also cut him off from distractions and allow him to concentrate totally on his work.

In 1919, Marconi bought from the British Admiralty a 60 m (220 ft) yacht that had been built in Scotland for an Austrian aristocrat, confiscated as enemy property during the war, and then used as a minesweeper. Marconi had her refitted and renamed *Elettra*. With a crew of 30, she could sail almost anywhere in the world. From that time on, Marconi regarded it as being as much his home as anywhere on shore. The "great white yacht" became another example of his larger-than-life way of doing things.

The 700 tonne *Elettra* at anchor. In 1922, Marconi sailed to New York so he could address the American Institute of Electrical Engineers.

Marconi's laboratory aboard *Elettra*, packed with advanced equipment, was a floating research institute to match any university.

Marconi often used to entertain large numbers of guests aboard *Elettra*, but the radio laboratory was an "off-limits" area where he could be alone with his work.

The Statesman

The coming of peace in 1918 was not a happy time for Marconi. As a member of the Italian delegation at the Paris Peace Conference, he felt that his country's wartime sacrifices were insufficiently recognized by the other powers. This may have influenced his later decision to join Benito Mussolini's Italian **Fascist** party, which aimed to restore Italian national pride.

Shortly after the disappointments of 1918 came the news of his mother's sudden death. Marconi was in Italy at the time and could not reach London in time for the funeral. And, finally, his marriage began to give way under the strain of his prolonged absences and his constant interest in other women. In 1923 his wife at last asked him for a divorce so that she could remarry. Marconi made the necessary arrangements and they remained on good terms, taking a common pride

Marconi with his second wife and their daughter, Elettra.

in their children.

Marconi's scientific interest had now turned to short-wave wireless, which needed far less power to send transmissions and so would be much cheaper to build and operate. Throughout 1922 and 1923, Marconi and his English-based team worked on the many technical problems involved in a short-wave transmission system.

The British government, meanwhile, dragged its feet over the long-discussed question of an Imperial Wireless Scheme, which would link the various countries of the British Empire together by means of a network of long-wave transmitters. In 1924, Marconi dropped a bombshell: he proposed an entirely new scheme, based on short-wave stations, which, of course, only the Marconi Company could operate. The British government accepted the Marconi proposal.

The acceptance of the short-wave scheme was a triumph for the Marconi Company but it presented them with a tough and risky challenge. Marconi's research team had conducted a promising series of experiments. But could these, in practice, provide the technology needed for a reliable commercial service? The contract signed by the company obliged it to accept all the costs involved if the system failed to live up to its promise. Failure could mean ruin.

All Marconi's hard work, daring and faith were finally rewarded in October 1926, when the first successful test transmissions were sent between Britain and Canada. A chain of stations was then swiftly established in South Africa, India, Australia, the United States and South America. Marconi's youthful dream of a world-wide network of communications had at last come true.

Marconi married for the second time in 1927. His bride, Cristina Bezzi-Scali, was the beautiful daughter of a Roman aristocrat and Vatican official, and less than half Marconi's age. As a result of his marriage, Marconi became a Roman Catholic. The couple had another daughter whom they named Elettra.

By now Marconi was visibly slowing down. He suffered from **angina** and had repeated heart attacks. He took a far less active part in the affairs of the Marconi Company. But he was still keen to experiment and was very interested in the possibilities of using **microwave** radiations. He directed a research programme to study their use in detecting ships and aircraft. In other words, this was a form of **radar**.

In 1934, he staged his last major public demonstration of the possibilities of a new technology — and it was as theatrical as anything he had ever done. His yacht *Elettra* steamed into the Italian harbour of Sestri Levante at full speed, with all the windows on her bridge blacked out. No disaster ensued. The secret of her blind but safe navigation through the treacherous channel was a guidance beam from an ultra-high-frequency beacon positioned on cliffs high above the harbour.

Marconi still insisted on enjoying his fame, and in 1933–4 undertook a triumphant world tour which involved attending "Marconi Day" at the Chicago Exposition. He was entertained by President Roosevelt

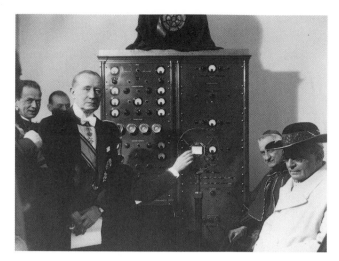

Marconi inaugurates a radio link between the Vatican and the Pope's summer residence, Castel Gandolfo.

A British microwave tower (1966), part of a nationwide network for telecommunications.

at the White House, and stayed with the film star Mary Pickford in Hollywood. He was also received by the Emperor in Japan, before returning to Italy via China and India. It was scarcely a restful journey. In September, when he was in Venice to address a conference on the possible medical applications of microwaves, he suffered a severe heart attack. Nevertheless, by November he was back in England to attend a royal wedding. A further heart attack followed. Then, in 1935, Italy invaded Abyssinia. Mussolini asked Marconi to defend this action by visiting those countries that disapproved and explaining why Italy had done so.

Marconi had already become a Senator, and had joined Mussolini's Fascist party as long ago as 1923. Mussolini had heaped honours on him, including the title of Marchese (Marquis). Privately, however,

Mussolini with a youthful admirer. Marconi became disillusioned by him.

work in these words: "What other men had been content to prove impossible, he accomplished; and this is surely greatness."

Still full of energy — Marconi (above) **aboard the *Elettra* with his second wife, but failing health had begun to take its toll.**

Marconi had come to have doubts about the Fascist régime and he now thought the Italian dictator would "listen only to what he wants to hear." But, as a true Italian patriot, he insisted on carrying out the exhausting foreign travel that Mussolini was now asking of him.

During the last eighteen months of Marconi's life, he grew steadily more feeble. He put his family and business affairs in order and resigned himself to death, which came on 20 July, 1937. In a unique tribute to his achievements, wireless stations throughout the world observed a two-minute silence. The airwaves were for a brief instant as silent as before he conquered them. The London *Times* summed up his

Find Out More ...

Important Books

Audio and Radio by J. Hawkins (Usborne, 1982)

Guglielmo Marconi by Keith Geddes (Her Majesty's Stationery Office, 1974)

Marconi by W.P. Jolly (Constable, 1972)

My Father, Marconi by Degna Marconi (Muller, 1962)

Radio and British Telecom (British Telecom Education Service, 1979)

Radio and Radar by Frank Young (Franklin Watts, 1984)

Important Addresses

The Science Museum
Exhibition Road, South Kensington
London SW7

Important Dates

1874 Birth of Guglielmo Marconi in Bologna, Italy

1894 Begins experiments in wireless telegraphy

1896 Travels to London; patents wireless and demonstrates it to GPO and military officials

1897 Transmits radio signals across Bristol Channel and establishes his wireless company

1898 Reports Kingstown regatta and opens Chelmsford radio factory

1899 Makes first international transmission

1900 Establishes Marconi International Marine Communication Company

1901 Makes successful transatlantic transmission

1905 Marries Beatrice O'Brien

1907 Inaugurates commercial transatlantic wireless service

1909 Awarded Nobel Prize for Physics

1910 Proposes an "Imperial Wireless Scheme"

1912 "Marconi Scandal"; loses an eye in car crash

1914 Appointed an Italian Senator

1915 Adviser to Italian armed forces

1917 Good-will mission to USA

1919 Delegate at Paris Peace Conference; buys yacht *Elettra*

1923 Joins Fascist party

1924 Divorces Beatrice; develops short-wave radio

1927 Marries Cristina Bezzi-Scali

1933–4 Goes on world tour

1935 Undertakes last diplomatic mission for Italian government

1937 20 July, dies in Rome

Glossary

Aerial Wire or rod set up to receive and/or send out radio waves.

Angina Type of heart disease.

Attaché Junior member of staff working for an ambassador.

Coherer Piece of apparatus that detects electric waves.

Earth Electrical connection to the earth, usually made by wire.

Fascist Belonging to a right-wing political party, such as Mussolini's Fascist party which was in power in Italy from 1922–43.

Frequency The number of electric voltage cycles per second.

Microwave Electromagnetic radiation with a very short wavelength and a high frequency. Microwaves are used in electronic communication and as a way of cooking food.

Morse code Dot and dash sound code used to send telegraph messages.

Neutral In wartime, a neutral country does not take part in the war, and supports neither side.

Patent Official document that gives an inventor the right to his or her invention so that nobody else can copy it.

Radar System that bounces radio waves off objects so that you can "see" where they are even when they are out of sight.

Radio Way of sending messages using radio waves, not wires.

Radio waves Electromagnetic waves that travel at the speed of light.

Spit Machine that turns meat over a fire so that it cooks evenly.

Static Electrical disturbance in the atmosphere that interferes with radio communication.

Strategic To do with planning the movement of troops in wartime.

Telegraph Method of sending messages, using sounds sent along wires.

Wireless Early name for radio.

Index

Bell, Alexander Graham 6
Bezzi-Scali, Cristina 27
Bologna University 7
Branly Coherer 7
Braun, K.F. 17

Cape Cod, Mass. 14
Chelmsford 20
Clerk-Maxwell, James 6
Clifden 16-17
Colour photographs 6
Crystal receiver 11

Electromagnetic waves 6
Elettra 24-5

Fascist party 26

Hertz, Heinrich 6
Hertzian waves 6

Imperial Wireless Scheme 17,20
Isaacs, Godfrey 16
Isle of Wight 13
Italian Naval Academy 4
Italian navy 10,11

Kemp 11,18

Leghorn Technical Institute 4
Lodge, Oliver 7
London 8,9,11,20

Marconi Company, 14, 18-19
Marconi Guglielmo
    birth 4
    schooling 4
    early experiments 4
    interest in physics 4
    interest in chemistry 4
    mother's influence 4,5
    learns Morse code 5
    early interest in electricity 5
    wireless telegraphy 7
    experiments with coherer 8
    father's influence 8
    moves to London 8
    files patent 9
    demonstrates invention 9
    kites and balloons 10

military service 10
assistant naval attaché 11
ship to shore experiments 11,13,16
made director 11
meets Queen Victoria 12
first international radio transmission 13
transatlantic experiments 14-15,16,27
marries Beatrice O'Brien 16
birth of daughter 17
honours received 17,22,28,29
first wireless stations 18
sets up Chelmsford factory 20
active service 20
Paris Peace Conference 26
divorces wife 26
Marries Cristina Bezzi-Scali 27
shortwave stations 27
radar 28
becomes Senator 28
death 29
Microwaves 28
Morse code 5
Mussolini 26,28-29

Nobel prize 18

O'Brien, Beatrice 16

Poldhu, Cornwall 13,14
Poole, Dorset 13
Preece, William 9
Professor Righi 5,7

Queen Victoria 12

Radar 28

Salisbury Plain 9,10
Solari, Luigi 4
Spezia 11
SS Lusitania 19

Titanic 19

Villa Grifone 4,7
Von Helmholtz, Hermann 6

War Office 9
Wireless Telegraph & Signal Company Limited 11
World War I 20-21

Picture Acknowledgements

The publishers would like to thank the following for their kind permission to reproduce their photographs in this book:
The Mansell Collection, cover, 12,19 (bottom), 23; The Marconi Company Limited, Frontispiece 4,8 (bottom), 9,10,11 (top), 13,14,15,16,17,18,19 (top), 20,21,22,24,25,26,27,28 (top), 29 (centre), 29 (bottom), 31; Mary Evans, 6 (left), 7; The Wayland Picture Library, 5,6 (right), 8 (top), 11 (bottom), 28 (bottom), 29 (top).